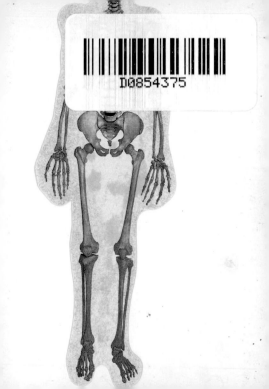

D0854375

A PARRAGON BOOK

Published by Parragon Book Service Ltd,
Units 13-17, Avonbridge Trading Estate, Atlantic Road,
Avonmouth, Bristol BS11 9QD

Produced by The Templar Company plc,
Pippbrook Mill, London Road, Dorking,
Surrey RH4 1JE

Written by Robert Snedden
Series Editor Robert Snedden
Designed by Mark Summersby
Illustrated by Julian Baker

Printed and bound in the UK

ISBN 0 7525 1683 3

HUMAN
BODY

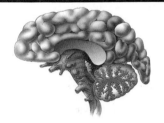

||| •PARRAGON• |||

CONTENTS

INTRODUCTION

The human body is a fascinating and complex living thing. Throughout your life, your body performs a multitude of tasks, often entirely without your conscious control. Every day your heart will beat around 100,000 times, and you won't even have to think about it! Once you have completed the act of chewing and swallowing food the rest of your digestive system will swing into action to extract the nutrients, and again you won't have to concentrate on doing it.

The human body starts life as a single cell – an egg, produced by a female, fertilized by a single sperm, produced by a male. From this simple beginning will develop all of the variety of tissues and organ systems that make up your body: skeleton; muscles; respiratory system – the windpipe, lungs and diaphragm; circulatory system – the heart, blood and blood vessels; digestive system – the stomach, intestines, pancreas and liver; nervous system – the brain, spinal cord and nerves; the senses – eyes, ears, tongue, nose and skin; and the reproductive system that starts the whole process off again!

This book will look at the major parts of the body individually and together to examine the ways in which the systems of the healthy body are coordinated with all the parts functioning together seamlessly. To see something you need your eyes and your brain, to digest food and get the nourishment from it around your body several organs need to work together, including your stomach, intestines, liver, pancreas, blood vessels and heart.

Clearly, such a complex construction is bound to go wrong from time to time and very few of us can claim to be in perfect health. However, the healthier you are the better your body will be able to function and there is always something you can do to improve matters. A good diet is crucial – poor nutrition invariably leads to poor health. Raising your overall level of fitness by taking regular exercise will improve your ability to fight off any illnesses you may succumb to. At the same time it is also important to get sufficient rest since it is during these quiet periods that the body carries out its running repairs. Too much alcohol will damage the liver, a vitally important organ that you can't live without, and smoking, with the cocktail of carcinogens in cigarette smoke, is a bad idea at any time.

Such an amazing thing as your human body deserves to be respected and looked after. If nothing else, it's the only one you'll have, it has to last you a lifetime and, when it goes, you go too!

THE SKELETON

The skeleton is a support-ing framework for the rest of the body, giving protection to vital organs and providing a place for muscles to be attached and to pull against. At birth, a child has around 350 bones but through life many of these fuse together and adults have only 206 bones.

The bones that make up the skeleton range in size from the tiny ossicles in the ear (the smallest is just 3mm/0.12in long) to the thigh bone or femur, stretching from hip to knee. Your hands are the most complicated parts of your skeleton and contain fully a quarter of the bones in your body.

Your skeleton is very much a living part of your body. Bone can grow and renew itself, repairing any damage or growing to meet the stresses and strains of work.

Tibia

Carpals

Metatarsals

Metacarpals

Phalanges

Phalanges

Tarsals

Fibula

Patella

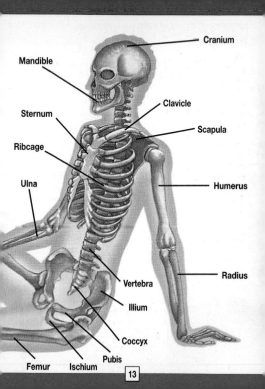

Cranium

Mandible

Clavicle

Sternum

Scapula

Ribcage

Ulna

Humerus

Vertebra

Illium

Radius

Coccyx

Femur Ischium Pubis

13

BONE STRUCTURE

Compact bone tissue is one of the hardest parts of the human body. A cross-section through compact bone shows a series of bunched-up concentric layers of bony tissue like closely packed cylinders. These layers are made up of a firm mixture of proteins and calcium salts. The proteins give the bone flexibility and the calcium makes it hard. Through a microscope, we can see that each cylinder has a central channel running through it. This carries nerves and capillaries to bring essential nutrients to the living bone. In between

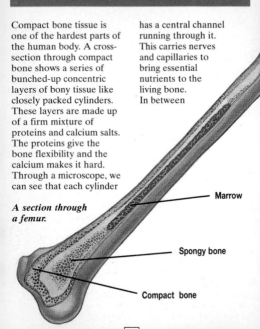

A section through a femur.

Marrow

Spongy bone

Compact bone

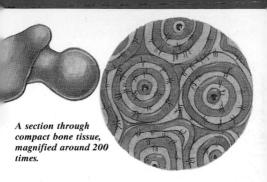

A section through compact bone tissue, magnified around 200 times.

the layers of bony tissue there are spaces that contain bone cells. Tiny channels connect these cells to the blood supply in the central canal.

Many of the larger bones, such as the femur and other long bones, are hollow along part of their length and filled with yellow bone marrow. This acts as a reserve of fat for the rest of the body.

Spongy bone tissue, found particularly in the ribs, vertebrae and pelvis, has lots of spaces that are filled by red bone marrow. This produces millions of blood cells for the body's circulatory system.

A protective skin of tough connective tissue covers and protects all bones. It is to this connective tissue that the tendons of muscles are attached.

JOINTS

If all your bones were joined rigidly together you wouldn't be able to move, so where one bone meets another they are hinged in some way to allow movement. Tough fibrous tissues called ligaments bind the bones together.

The joints at the knees, fingers and elbows open and close like the hinges on a door. The knee also swivels around to some degree, so the foot can be turned from side to side. This type of joint allows the greatest movement.

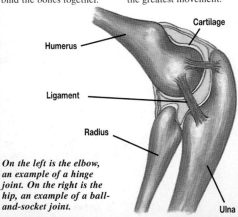

Cartilage

Humerus

Ligament

Radius

Ulna

On the left is the elbow, an example of a hinge joint. On the right is the hip, an example of a ball-and-socket joint.

The hip joint is a ball-and-socket type joint, allowing all round movement. The ball at the end of the femur fits snugly into a socket in the hip bone. As well as giving smooth movement the cartilage ensures a tight fit between the bones. The ligaments holding the bones together are particularly strong. As in all joints, slippery cartilage between the bone surfaces allows them to move easily. The cartilage in a joint also acts like a shock absorber. Between the layers of cartilage there is a substance called synovial fluid, secreted by the synovial membrane, which provides extra lubrication.

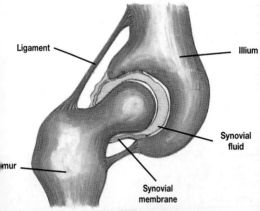

Ligament

Illium

Synovial fluid

Femur

Synovial membrane

THE MUSCLES

Muscles make up about half of your body weight. Some muscles, such as those in the heart, work automatically without conscious control, others such as the ones that move your limbs, move when you want them to.

Muscles move by contracting and pulling – they cannot push – so the ones that move your skeleton work in pairs. For example, the biceps muscle pulls your forearm up and the triceps pulls it back down again. There are around 640 muscles in the body, moving various parts of the skelton. The biggest of these is the gluteus maximus, in the thighs and buttocks, which straightens the thigh, and the smallest is the stapedius in the inner ear, which pulls on one of the tiny ossicles.

Some of the integrated system of muscles that is used to move your body.

18

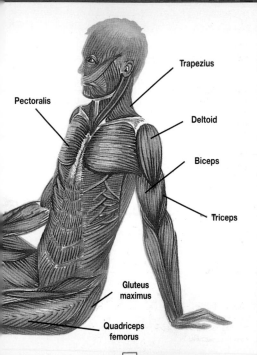

Trapezius

Pectoralis

Deltoid

Biceps

Triceps

Gluteus
maximus

Quadriceps
femorus

MUSCLE TYPES

There are three types of muscle in the human body. Voluntary or skeletal muscles are made up of bundles of fibres surrounded by connective tissue. Involuntary, or smooth, muscle, the sort that is found in the digestive system, is made up of spindle-shaped muscle cells that fit together into a sheet of muscle. Again there is connective tissue and blood vessels between the muscle cells. Cardiac muscle, the sort that makes up the heart, is similar to voluntary muscle, but the cells are arranged like a net of branched fibres with connections between the individual cells. This cell network allows the heart muscle to contract and relax swiftly and smoothly without stopping all through your life.

SKELETAL MUSCLE

SMOOTH MUSCLE

CARDIAC MUSCLE

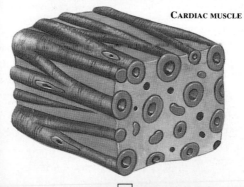

THE SKIN

The skin is the largest organ in your body and it performs many different functions. It protects against injury and attack by bacteria, fungi, viruses, and parasites. The skin also protects against ultra-violet radiation by producing the pigment melanin, which can range in colour from yellow to black. The skin controls body temperature in various ways, as well. Heat loss through the skin occurs through transfer from the capillaries running through the skin to the cooler cells of the outer layer, or epidermis, of the skin. The amount of heat lost is adjusted by either contracting or dilating (opening up) the blood vessels. The evaporation of sweat, produced by glands in the

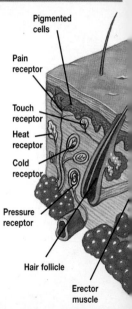

Pigmented cells

Pain receptor

Touch receptor

Heat receptor

Cold receptor

Pressure receptor

Hair follicle

Erector muscle

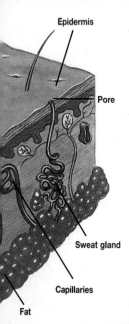

Epidermis

Pore

Sweat gland

Capillaries

Fat

skin, also cools the skin. A layer of insulating fat on the undersurface of the skin helps to keep heat in the inside of the body.

Another important role played by the skin is to provide information about your environment. Under the surface of your skin there are several types of specialized nerve endings. Five distinct sensations can be detected by the nerves in the skin, including touch, pain, heat, cold and pressure. Although they look very similar, each nerve ending can respond to only one of the five basic types of sensation.

A cross-section through a portion of skin showing some of the sensory and other structures.

THE RESPIRATORY SYSTEM

When you take a breath air first passes into the nose or mouth, then through the throat and the larynx and then into the trachea (windpipe). The nose, mouth and throat are all well-supplied with blood vessels and this brings the air to body temperature and humidity. The trachea splits into two bronchi and these in turn split to supply each of the five lobes that make up each lung. Within each lobe the branches divide into yet finer branches, the smallest of which are called bronchioles.

Bronchioles that are more than 1mm in diameter have walls made of smooth muscle that expands and contracts and are supported by rings of cartilage. The inner surfaces of the bronchioles are covered by cells with tiny hair-like projections, called cilia, and by mucus producing goblet cells. Particles that are breathed into the bronchioles are carried up and out on the mucus by the beating of the cilia, eventually reaching the throat, where they are cleared.

The bronchioles end in pouches of tiny air sacs, each sac consisting of a cluster of alveoli where gas exchange with the bloodstream takes place (see page 28). The cilia and goblet cells gradually disappear from bronchioles smaller than 1mm in diameter and the smallest airways and the entrance to the alveoli supported by a network of connective tissue.

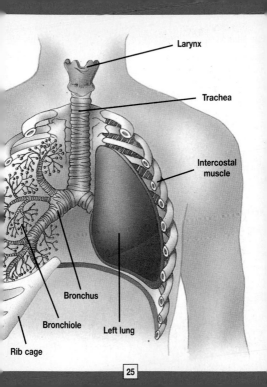

Larynx

Trachea

Intercostal
muscle

Bronchus

Bronchiole

Left lung

Rib cage

BREATHING

When you breathe in, intercostal muscles between your ribs contract and lift the ribs up and out; at the same time muscles around your diaphragm, the sheet of connective tissue that separates the chest cavity from the abdominal cavity, pull it flat. Both these actions make your chest cavity larger, lowering the pressure inside it, and air flows into the lungs.

When you breathe out, another set of intercostal muscles brings the ribcage down and in, and the

When the chest cavity expands the pressure inside is reduced and air flows in.

muscles around the diaphragm relax, and it returns to a dome shape. The chest cavity is reduced in size, increasing the pressure inside, and air flows out of the lungs. Only the diaphragm moves while you breathe when at rest. It is only when you are exercising or take a deep breath that the intercostal muscles are used and your ribcage rises and falls. The lungs are never emptied of air. There is always about 1.5 litres of air in an adult's lungs. This is called residual air. The volume of air that is breathed in and out is called tidal air and amounts to around half a litre at a time when a person is at rest.

When the chest cavity contracts the pressure inside increases and air flows out.

INSIDE THE LUNGS

Each lung contains almost half a billion tiny sacs, called alveoli, each of which is less than 1mm (0.04 in) in diameter. Each alveolus is surrounded by a network of tiny capillaries. When the blood cells in the capillar-

Every bronchiole ends in a bunch of tiny alveoli.

ies pass by the alveoli an exchange of gases takes place. The wall of the capillary is only a single cell thick so the blood cells are as close to the air sac as possible. Oxygen from the air you breathe in passes across the wall of the air sac to combine with haemoglobin, the red pigment that gives blood its colour, in the red blood

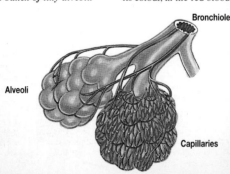

Bronchiole

Alveoli

Capillaries

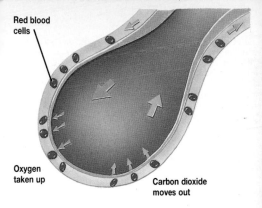

Red blood cells

Oxygen taken up

Carbon dioxide moves out

An exchange of gases takes place across the thin wall of the alveolus.

cells. At the same time carbon dioxide moves from the blood and across the wall into the alveolus to be breathed out.

These capillaries arise from the multiple branch-

ing of the pulmonary artery, which carries blood that is depleted of oxygen from the heart. As the capillaries leave the lung they rejoin to form the superior and inferior pulmonary veins, which return oxygenated blood to the heart, which pumps it to the other organs of the body.

BLOOD

The liquid part of blood, in which the blood cells move, is called plasma. It is 90 per cent water with the remainder being made up of proteins, minerals, hormones and a mixture of food and wastes.

There are two classes of cell in the blood. Red blood cells are made in the red bone marrow. They carry the red pigment haemoglobin, which binds with oxygen in the lungs to transport it around the body. Red blood cells live for about four months before being reabsorbed in the liver or spleen. There are two types of white blood cells. Phagocytes, also made in the red bone marrow, engulf and destroy invading bacteria in the body. Lymphocytes, made by the lymphatic system, are spherical. They manufacture antibodies, another of the bodies defences against infection. Finally, there are the platelets, which are involved in clotting.

Red blood cells carry haemoglobin, a red pigment that binds with oxygen.

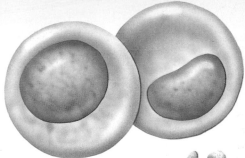

Lymphocytes produce antibodies, one of the body's defences against infection.

Platelets are involved in blood clotting.

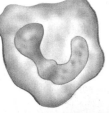

Phagocytes can engulf and destroy invading bacteria.

CIRCULATION

The circulatory system consists of the heart, arteries, veins and capillaries. Arteries carry blood away from the heart and veins carry blood to the heart. Capillaries are very fine vessels connecting arteries to veins.

The pulmonary artery carries blood from the heart to the lungs. Like all the body's arteries, it divides into smaller branches, called arterioles. These carry blood to the network of capillaries surrounding the alveoli of the lungs. These join together to form venules, which form the pulmonary vein, taking oxygenated blood back to the heart.

The oxygenated blood is then pumped into the aorta, which runs the length of the torso, with arteries branching off to the head, arms, digestive tract, kidneys, legs and the tissues of all other parts of the body. The blood

A complex system of blood vessels supplies all parts of the body.

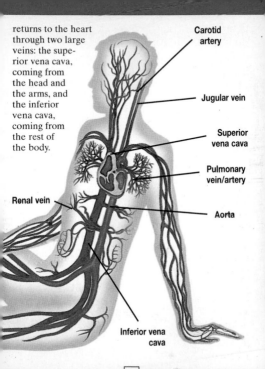

returns to the heart through two large veins: the superior vena cava, coming from the head and the arms, and the inferior vena cava, coming from the rest of the body.

Carotid artery

Jugular vein

Superior vena cava

Pulmonary vein/artery

Aorta

Renal vein

Inferior vena cava

THE HEART

The heart lies to the left of centre in the chest cavity, protected by the ribcage. It is a powerful, muscular pump that moves the blood around inside your body. It is divided into four chambers, a left and right atrium and a left and right ventricle. The thin-walled atria are collecting chambers and are found in the top half of the heart. The atria receive blood from the veins – the left atrium receives oxygenated blood from the pulmonary veins. When it is full the blood is pushed through a valve into the left ventricle. The thick-walled ventricles in the lower half of the heart are the pumping chambers. They push blood back out through the arteries. The walls of the ventricles are about three times thicker than those of the atria. When the left ventricle is full it contracts, pushing blood through the aorta to carry oxygenated blood to the body's tissues. The right atrium receives deoxygenated blood from the rest of the body through the inferior and superior vena cava. The blood flows from the atrium through another valve into the right ventricle. From the right ventricle it is pushed back out to the lungs through the pulmonary artery.

The heart is the pump and switching point for the body's circulation system, directing deoxygenated blood to the lungs and pumping oxygenated blood to the rest of the body.

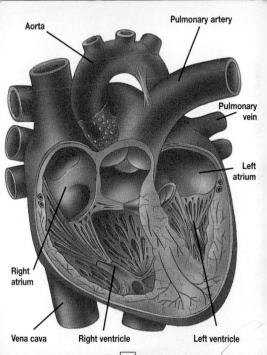

Aorta

Pulmonary artery

Pulmonary vein

Left atrium

Right atrium

Vena cava

Right ventricle

Left ventricle

HEARTBEAT

A heartbeat is a contraction of the heart, which forces blood through the arteries to all parts of the body. On average, the heart of an adult human at rest will beat about 70 times per minute. Very fit people, such as trained athletes, may have resting heart rates as low as 40 beats per minute. During exercise, or when a person is frightened or excited, the heart rate may

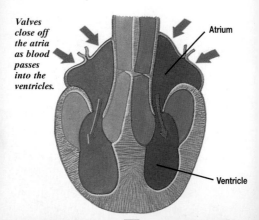

Valves close off the atria as blood passes into the ventricles.

Atrium

Ventricle

increase to more than 150 beats per minute. This faster than normal heart rate is called tachycardia. Bradycardia, on the other hand, is a rate of less than 60 beats per minute.

The heart rate is controlled by a part of the heart called the sinoatrial node, or pacemaker, a knot of tissue in the heart muscle. The pacemaker is controlled by two sets of nerves and sets off a wave of muscle contractiont.

In each heartbeat blood flows into the atria from the rest of the body, passes into the ventricles and is then pumped out.

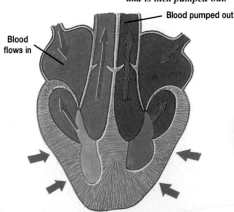

Blood pumped out

Blood flows in

THE DIGESTIVE SYSTEM

Food first enters the digestive system by way of the mouth. Here, the first stage of its breakdown begins with chewing. The chewed up food, or bolus, passes through the oesophagus and enters the stomach where it is liquefied by a mixture of hydrochloric acid and the enzyme pepsin released by the stomach wall. The contents of the stomach are pushed out bit by bit by a muscular pumping motion called peristalsis into the duodenum, the first section of the small intestine. The small intestine is where most nutrients are absorbed into the body. A duct from the pancreas and the gall bladder introduces a variety of chemicals into the duodenum, including bicarbonate, which neutralises the stomach acid, enzymes to break down proteins and carbohydrates, and bile salts to absorb fat. Peristalsis moves the semi-liquid food mass, called chyme, into the next section of the small intestine, the jejunum, where most of the digested carbohydrates, proteins, water, vitamins and minerals are absorbed. In the last third of the small intestine, the ileum, fat, vitamins A, D, E and K, vitamin B12 and bile salts are absorbed. The indigestible remains of the food, together with some fluid, pass into the colon where more water is removed and the chyme is thickened to form stools. Further peristalsis moves this into the rectum for evacuation.

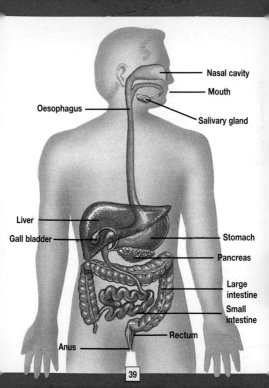

Nasal cavity

Mouth

Salivary gland

Oesophagus

Liver

Gall bladder

Stomach

Pancreas

Large intestine

Small intestine

Rectum

Anus

39

THE MOUTH

When you take a mouthful of food your tongue, teeth and salivary glands work together to begin the process of breaking it down. The salivary glands produce digestive enzymes that start off the process of food digestion. The largest salivary glands are in the cheeks, others are found beneath the tongue and in the neck. The sight, smell and even the thought of food stimulates the production of saliva which is discharged through a series of ducts into the mouth. Saliva helps the taste buds to taste food, keep the mouth moist for speaking and cleanse the mouth of the carbohydrates that can cause tooth decay.

Chewing food breaks it up into smaller pieces increasing its surface area and giving the digestive enzymes more to work on. When the food has been thoroughly mixed with saliva the tongue moves the food to the back of the mouth, then the lump is swallowed and passes into the oesophagus to begin the next stage of its journey through the digestive system. The epiglottis covers the entrance to the windpipe to prevent choking when you swallow.

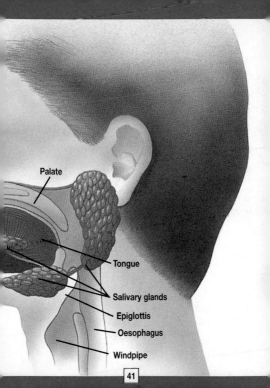

Palate

Tongue

Salivary glands

Epiglottis

Oesophagus

Windpipe

TEETH

The first of the two sets of teeth, called the milk teeth or primary dentition, emerges between the ages of six months and two years. There are 20 milk teeth – 4 central incisors, 4 lateral incisors, 4 canines, and 8 molars. Between the ages of six and thirteen these are replaced by the 32 permanent or adult-teeth – 4 central incisors, 4 lateral incisors, 4 cuspids, 8 bicuspids (premolars), and 12 molars. The upper teeth and lower teeth are shaped so that they fit together when the jaws are closed. The molars and premolars have large surfaces with points and grooves and fit together extremely well.

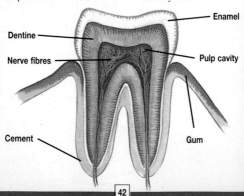

Enamel

Dentine

Nerve fibres

Pulp cavity

Cement

Gum

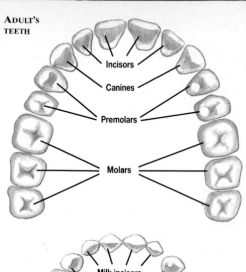

ADULT'S
TEETH

Incisors

Canines

Premolars

Molars

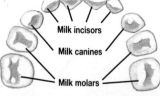

Milk incisors

Milk canines

Milk molars

CHILD'S
TEETH

TOOTH TYPES

An adult has four types of teeth, canines, incisors, premolars and molars (children do not have any premolars), and each type is suited to a particular task.

The incisors, at the front of the mouth, are shaped like chisels and have sharp edges. They are used for cutting and biting food. They have a single long root.

The canines are the sharp, pointed teeth to either side of the incisors. The top of the point of the canine is called the cusp. Canines are used to tear

Canine

Incisor

food. Like incisors, they have a single long root.

Premolars, next to the canines, have two points, or cusps. They are used for grinding and tearing food. Premolars have a double root.

Finally, at the back of the mouth, there are the molars. Molars can have up to five cusps. They are used for grinding, crushing and chewing food. Molars have a triple root, anchoring them firmly in the jaw. The final molars, the wisdom teeth, right at the back of the mouth, are the last of the permanent teeth to appear.

The differing shapes of the four tooth types suits them to their different functions.

Premolar

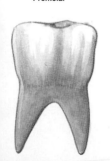

Molar

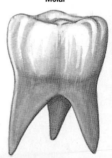

THE STOMACH

The stomach is a bottle-shaped organ less than 20cm (8 ins) long. It aids digestion by mechanically and chemically breaking down the food you eat. It can swell up to accommodate large meals.

During a meal the stomach secretes gastric juices, consisting of acid, mucus and other chemicals. The mucus lubricates the stomach wall and protects it from damage by food as well as preventing the acid from digesting the stomach! The hydrochloric acid acts together with the enzyme pepsin to digest meat and other proteins. The acid also kills any bacteria that enter the stomach along with food.

Sphincter muscles at either end seal food in the stomach. For the next hour or so the stomach wall ripples with peristaltic waves, mixing the food with the gastric juices and continuing the process of breaking it down.

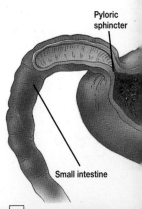

Pyloric sphincter

Small intestine

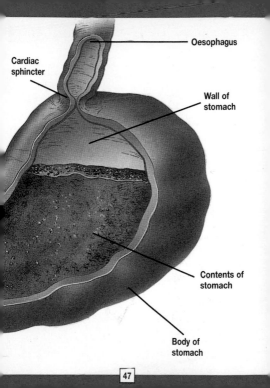

Oesophagus

Cardiac sphincter

Wall of stomach

Contents of stomach

Body of stomach

THE SMALL INTESTINE

The small intestine is the part of the digestive system that comes after the stomach. This is where most of the digestion and absorption of nutrients takes place. Very little in the way of digestible substances reaches the large intestine. The small intestine is a tightly coiled, hollow tube about 5 metres (16.4 feet) in length with two distinct sections – the duodenum and the ileum. The duodenum produces hormones that cause the gall bladder to release bile, which aids in the digestion of fat, and stimulate the pancreas to release digestive enzymes. These are delivered to the small intestine via a common duct from the gall bladder and pancreas. The duodenum also produces

Gall bladder

hormones that inhibit the production of acid by the stomach after the stomach contents have passed into it. Intestinal juices, produced by cells in the wall of the intestine, contain enzymes that digest proteins and carbohydrates.

Most of the absorption of nutrients takes place in the ileum. The ileum is the longest section of the intestine and so offers a large area for absorption to occur. Over the page we will see how the microscopic structure of the ileum increases its surface area 600-fold.

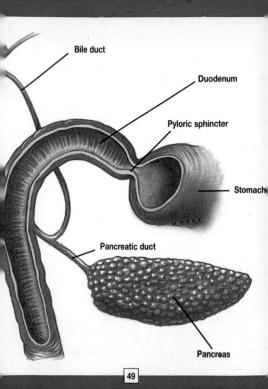

Bile duct

Duodenum

Pyloric sphincter

Stomach

Pancreatic duct

Pancreas

INSIDE THE INTESTINE

The small intestine has an enormous absorbing surface, called the mucosal epithelium. The surface area of the intestine is increased by millions of small finger-like projections called villi, which jut out into the intestine. The surface of each absorbing cell of the mucosa is also covered with microscopic brush-like projections called microvilli. This gives an absorbing surface that is equivalent in size to half a basketball court.

The surface layer of each villus is just a single cell thick. Within, there is a rich supply of blood capillaries into which the nutrients released by the break-down of food are absorbed across the

Villi

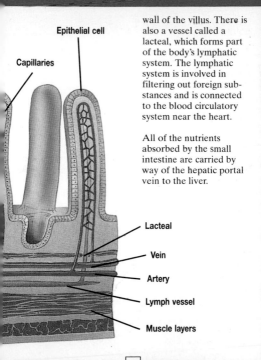

Epithelial cell

Capillaries

wall of the villus. There is also a vessel called a lacteal, which forms part of the body's lymphatic system. The lymphatic system is involved in filtering out foreign substances and is connected to the blood circulatory system near the heart.

All of the nutrients absorbed by the small intestine are carried by way of the hepatic portal vein to the liver.

Lacteal

Vein

Artery

Lymph vessel

Muscle layers

THE LIVER

The liver is the second-largest organ in the human body, after the skin. It is a spongy, reddish brown, consisting of two large lobes, and lies just below the diaphragm in the abdominal cavity. Three-quarters of the liver's blood supply comes via the hepatic portal vein, which transports digested nutrients and hormones from the intestines.

The liver's complex role in the body includes storing glucose absorbed by the intestines in the form of glycogen until it is needed. The amount of glucose released into the bloodstream by the liver is controlled by the pancreas. It also stores vitamins A and D and any surplus iron. The liver manufactures bile, which is used in digestion, by destroying old worn-out red blood cells. The bile manufactured in the liver passes down a series of ducts that connect to the common hepatic duct. This duct joins with the duct from the gall bladder and enters the duodenum. The liver also filters out impurities and toxic material from the blood and produces blood-clotting factors.

All of the activities that go on in the liver generate heat that helps to maintain the body at a suitable temperature.

One of the major functions of the liver is to act as a temporary storehouse for some of the nutrients absorbed by the intestines.

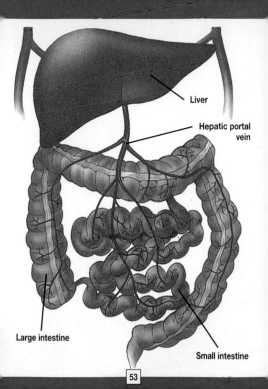

Liver

Hepatic portal vein

Large intestine

Small intestine

THE LARGE INTESTINE

The large intestine, or colon, performs the vital function of absorbing water and salts from the undigested food that passes into it from the small intestine. If the food mass passes through the colon too quickly not enough water is absorbed and the result is diarrhoea. This can lead to dehydration and loss of salts and can be a serious condition in infants, especially if it is prolonged. Constipation, on the other hand, results from an unusually slow passage of the food residues through the large intestine, leading to too much water being removed and resulting in the hard mass of undigested residues that is characteristic of constipation.

A normal bowel movement, or defecation, begins with sensory nerve receptors in the rectum being stimulated by the presence of faeces. The nerve receptors trigger a complex series of reflex actions that results in the sphincter muscles at the junction of the rectum and anus becoming relaxed, thus allowing defecation to take place unless the person makes a conscious effort to override the reflex.

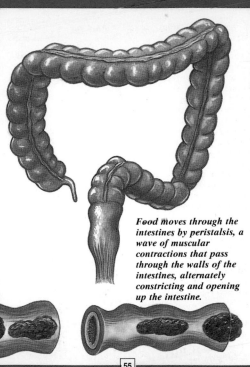

Food moves through the intestines by peristalsis, a wave of muscular contractions that pass through the walls of the intestines, alternately constricting and opening up the intestine.

The principal waste products produced by the body are carbon dioxide, which is expelled through the lungs, water and urea. Some water is retained by the body, some is lost by evaporation from the skin and lungs and the rest is excreted by the kidneys. Urea, a waste product of the liver, is also excreted via the kidneys.

The kidneys are together able to filter harmful and waste substances from more than a litre of blood every minute, a total of around 1500 litres every day. The blood supply to and from the kidneys travels through the renal arteries and veins. The filtered-out wastes are mixed with excess water to form a mixture called urine. The kidneys pro-

duce around 1.5 litres of urine a day, although this does depend on how much you drink. Urine is 96 per cent water with the rest of its volume being made up of urea, salt and other waste substances. It is transported from the kidneys through muscular tubes called ureters to the bladder. Up to about half a litre of urine can be stored in the bladder. The bladder is emptied through a tube called a urethra, which is opened and closed by a sphincter muscle.

Waste material is filtered from the blood by the kidneys and stored in the bladder with excess water for eventual evacuation via the urethra.

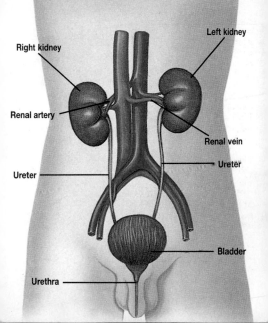

Right kidney

Left kidney

Renal artery

Renal vein

Ureter

Ureter

Bladder

Urethra

THE KIDNEYS

The kidneys are reddish-brown in colour, about 11cm (4.4 in) long and located just above the waist, on either side of the spine. Emerging from the kidney are the renal artery and renal vein, which take blood to and from the kidney, and the renal pelvis, a funnel-like structure in which waste urine from each kidney is collected before passing into the ureter, which extends downward into the bladder.

Inside the kidney there are over a million tiny nephrons. Each one has a cup-like capsule at one end into which liquid passes from a knot of tiny capillaries. The fluid passes along a long tube surrounded by a network of capillaries and any useful materials are reabsorbed into the bloodstream. When the fluid reaches the renal pelvis only waste urine is left. The amount of water in the body is controlled by adjusting what is reabsorbed by the nephrons.

Renal pelvis

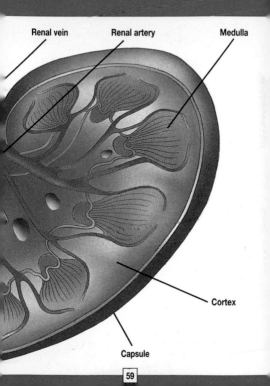

Renal vein

Renal artery

Medulla

Cortex

Capsule

THE PANCREAS

The pancreas is a long, thin organ measuring about 12-15cm (5-6 in) long that sits inside the curve of the small intestine and stretches behind the stomach. The cells of the pancreas involved in digestion produce secretions that contain three important digestive enzymes, trypsin, amylase and lipase. These digest proteins and fat and break down carbohydrates, such as

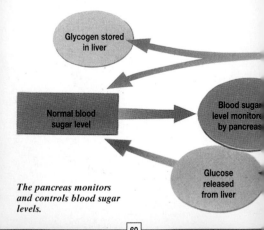

The pancreas monitors and controls blood sugar levels.

starch. Trypsin, the enzyme that splits proteins, only becomes active when it mixes with another enzyme in the duodenum.

The pancreas controls the level of sugars in the blood. Two hormones are released into the blood by groups of cells called the islets of Langerhans. These hormones regulate the amount of sugar released into the bloodstream by the liver. Insulin causes a decrease in blood sugar; glucagon increases it. A person lacking in islet cells may develop diabetes.

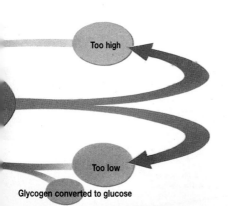

Too high

Too low

Glycogen converted to glucose

The nervous system is a highly organized collection of nerve cells, or neurons. There are three types of neuron: sensory neurons, which carry messages from the sense organs, motor neurons, which take messages from the central nervous system to the muscles and glands, and connecting neurons, which link sensory and motor neurons together. The central nervous system consists of the brain and spinal cord, and the remaining nervous tissue makes up the peripheral nervous system. The central nervous system coordinates the actions of the body as a whole. It receives information from the rest of the body and responds to it.

The autonomic nervous system, a part of the peripheral system, carries messages from the vital organs such as the heart and liver to the central nervous system. All of the actions produced by the autonomic system happen automatically without your conscious control.

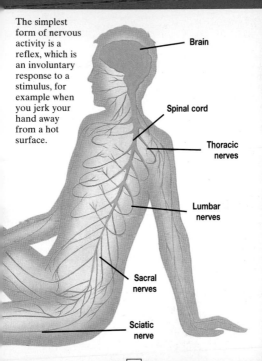

The simplest form of nervous activity is a reflex, which is an involuntary response to a stimulus, for example when you jerk your hand away from a hot surface.

Brain

Spinal cord

Thoracic nerves

Lumbar nerves

Sacral nerves

Sciatic nerve

THE BRAIN

The brain is the central control organ of the body, governing the functioning of the other organs. Sensory nerve cells continually feed information to the brain from all parts of the body. On average the brain weighs 390g (14 oz) at birth and reaches its average maximum weight of 1,315g (46 oz) at age 15. There are approximately 10 billion neurons in the human brain.

The brain is protected by the skull, by membranes, called meninges, and by the cerebrospinal fluid, which acts like a shock absorber between the brain and skull.

The main parts of the brain are the left and right cerebral hemispheres, the cerebellum and the

Right hemisphere of cerebrum

medulla oblongata. The cerebral hemispheres are responsible for a multitude of tasks, including controlling the voluntary muscles, interpreting the input from all the sensory organs, perceiving pain and temperature, intelligence, thinking and memory. The cerebellum controls balance and coordination and the medulla oblongata is responsible for involuntary actions, such as breathing, sneezing and swallowing.

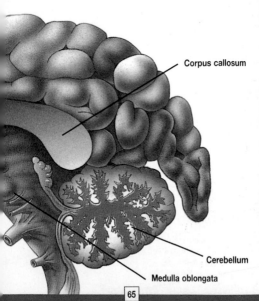

Corpus callosum

Cerebellum

Medulla oblongata

THE SPINE

The spinal cord conducts impulses between the brain and the rest of the body. There are thirty-one pairs of nerves extending from the spinal cord, which receive signals from other nerve cells in the central nervous system or in the peripheral nervous system.

The spinal cord is encased within three membranes called meninges and also protected by the spinal column. The skull, ribs, pelvis and various muscles and ligaments are all attached to the spine. The flexible part of the spine, or backbone, is made up of 24 separate vertebrae held together by strong ligaments: There are 7 cervical (neck) vertebrae, 12 thoracic vertebrae and 5 lumbar (lower back) vertebrae. Below this are the fused vertebrae that make up the sacrum and the coccyx, or tailbone. Each vertebra has two parts: the short, solid, cylindrical vertebral body or

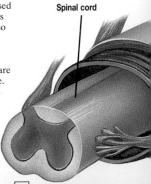

Spinal cord

centrum, and the vertebral, or neural, arch. In the centre of each arch is a large hole, the neural canal, which protects the spinal cord. Notches in the neural arches allow the spinal nerves to pass through from the cord. The vertebrae are separated from each other by pads of cartilage.

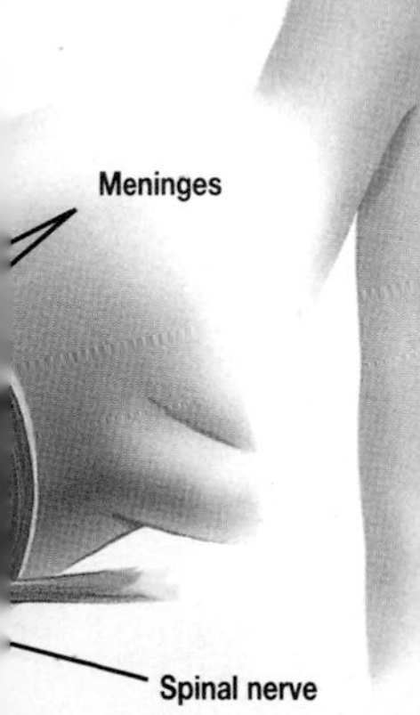

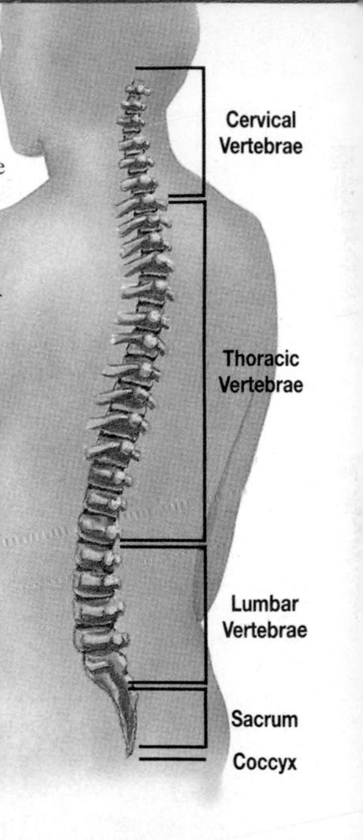

Cervical Vertebrae

Thoracic Vertebrae

Lumbar Vertebrae

Sacrum

Coccyx

Meninges

Spinal nerve

THE EYE

The adult human eye is a hollow globe roughly 2.5cm (1 in) in diameter. The eyeball is protected by a bony socket in the skull called the orbit. Further protection is provided by the eyelids, which also keep the surface clean and lubricated by spreading tear fluid, produced by the lacrimal glands, by blinking. The outer layer of the eyeball is composed of a transparent cornea at the front of the eye, which helps to focus light, and the sclera, the firm, white coat of the eye to which the six small muscles that move the eyeball are attached.

Behind the cornea is an opening called the pupil, which is surrounded by the iris. The iris opens and closes to regulate the

amount of light entering the eye. The light then passes through the lens, which focuses it on to the retina, a layer of light-sensitive cells at the back of

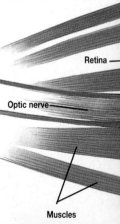

Retina

Optic nerve

Muscles

68

the eye. A circular arrangement of muscle and ligaments around the lens can change its shape, allowing near and far objects to be brought into focus. The cells in the retina send signals along the optic nerve to the brain, which interprets them.

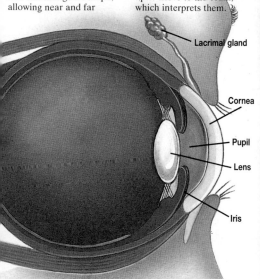

Lacrimal gland

Cornea

Pupil

Lens

Iris

THE EAR

The ears are the organs of hearing, and they are more than just the flaps of skin on either side of your head. The ear is made up of three parts: the outer ear, the middle ear, and the inner ear. The outer ear acts as a sound collector, directing it down a tube to the eardrum, or tympanic membrane, which separates the outer ear from the middle ear. Sounds make the eardrum vibrate and this movement is transferred to a smaller inner membrane by three small bones, called the auditory ossicles. The vibrations of the inner ear membrane move fluid contained within the snail-shaped cochlea, and this in turn vibrates hair cells that send signals down the auditory nerve to the brain where they are interpreted as sounds. A particularly loud noise makes muscles behind the eardrum contract to dampen the vibrations and prevent injury to the delicate membrane.

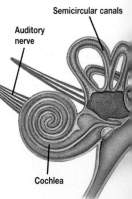

Semicircular canals

Auditory nerve

Cochlea

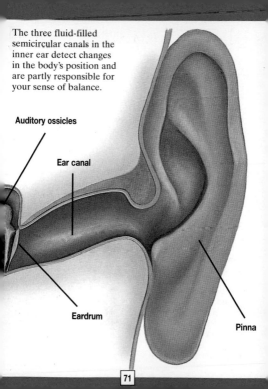

The three fluid-filled semicircular canals in the inner ear detect changes in the body's position and are partly responsible for your sense of balance.

Auditory ossicles

Ear canal

Eardrum

Pinna

THE TONGUE

In addition to helping in chewing, swallowing, and, of course, speaking, the tongue provides the sense of taste. There are numerous raised protuberances, called papillae, on the upper surface of the tongue. Adults have three types of papillae, the most numerous of which are the filiform papillae. Their function is mainly to provide friction to help in the movement of food. Scattered among them are the fungiform and vallate papillae. These are found mostly on the upper central surface of the tongue and contain the taste buds.

When you eat or drink chemicals dissolve in a layer of mucus on the surface of the tongue. The dissolved chemicals stimulate sensory cells or receptors, in the taste buds, which send signals to the brain. The tongue has four types of chemical receptor, sensitive to chemicals that are salty, bitter, sweet and sour. The salt receptors are concentrated at the tip of the tongue, the sweet receptors at the sides near the front, the sour receptors towards the back at the side, and the bitter on the upper rear surface.

The taste buds are too small to be seen on the tongue. Its rough surface allows food to be moved around inside the mouth.

Taste buds are concealed in pits in the tongue

THE NOSE

The nose is the site of the sense of smell. The nasal septum divides it into two passages, each of which begins with a nasal cavity. The lining of the cavity contains coarse hairs, sweat glands, oil-producing glands and cells that produce a watery mucus. There are also a number of large, thin-walled veins whose blood supply warms incoming air. Olfactory receptor cells are located at the top of the nasal cavity in the olfactory epithelium. Hair-like structures at their free surfaces detect odours from chemicals in the air dissolved in the mucus lining of the nose. Nerve cells convert the chemical information into sensory information and convey it first to the olfactory bulb on the other side of a thin section of the skull and then via the olfactory nerve to the higher centres of the brain.

Taste and smell work together to determine the flavour and palatability of foods and beverages and to signal the presence of dangerous gases and toxins. The sense of smell is vitally important in determining food flavours. During chewing and swallowing, odour-laden air is forced from the back of the mouth to the olfactory receptors producing flavour sensations that are almost entirely owing to the sense of smell. If your nose is blocked the flow of air to the olfactory receptors is prevented, resulting in your perception of the food's taste being reduced.

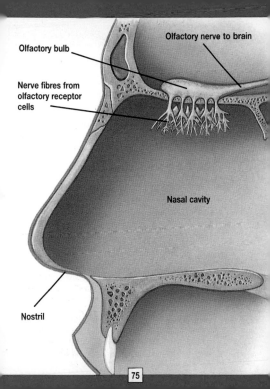

Olfactory nerve to brain

Olfactory bulb

Nerve fibres from
olfactory receptor
cells

Nasal cavity

Nostril

HORMONES

Hormones are the body's chemical messengers. They are released in minute amounts by the endocrine glands and transported via the circulatory system to target organs where they produce their effects. Hormones regulate conditions inside your body, control tissue development and reproduction and the body's responses to external and internal stimuli.

The most important endocrine glands in the body are: the pituitary, on the lower surface of the brain, often called the master gland because it controls the other glands; the thyroid, in the throat, which controls the metabolic rate of cells; the pancreas, in the abdomen, which controls blood sugar levels; the adrenals, above the kidneys, which help the body deal with stress and prepare for action; the testes, which control the development of male sexual characteristics; and the ovaries which control the female menstrual cycle.

Hormone production is controlled by a feedback loop. For example, the pituitary gland releases a hormone that stimulates the thyroid gland. The thyroid produces another hormone that is carried in the bloodstream back to the pituitary indicating that it has been activated. When the pituitary detects a high enough level of this hormone it shuts down its production of the thyroid stimulating hormone.

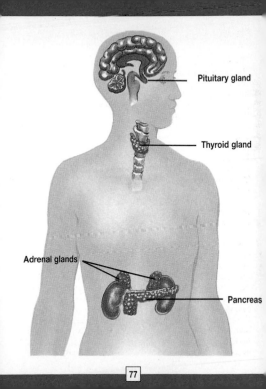

Pituitary gland

Thyroid gland

Adrenal glands

Pancreas

MALE REPRODUCTIVE ORGANS

The reproductive organs are where gametes, or sex cells, are made. The purpose of the male reproductive system is basically to produce and transport sperm cells, the male gametes. Sperm are produced in the testes (testicles). Within the scrotum, each testis is protected by a thick capsule, and inside this there are tightly coiled tubes, called the seminiferous tubules. If uncoiled these tubes would be almost 1.5km (a mile) in length. This is where the sperm cells develop. The male hormone testosterone is also produced in the testes in cells between the seminiferous tubules. This hormone circulates throughout the blood system and develops and maintains male sexual characteristics. The sperm cells move from the testis to the epididymis, where they are stored. The prostate gland, Cowper's gland and the seminal vesicle all supply food for the sperm. The mixture of sperm and its supply of nutrients is called semen.

Sperm production usually continues through all of adult life, and a man may father children into his seventies and eighties, although it does slow down in later years. Although the bladder empties through the urethra, a duct that runs through the length of the penis and by which sperm also leave the body, it is not considered part of the reproductive system.

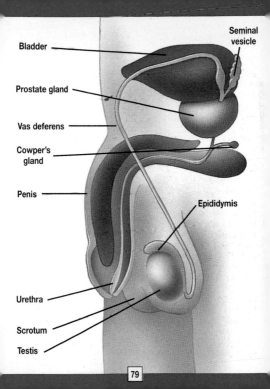

Seminal vesicle

Bladder

Prostate gland

Vas deferens

Cowper's gland

Penis

Epididymis

Urethra

Scrotum

Testis

FEMALE REPRODUCTIVE ORGANS

It is the function of the female ovaries to produce eggs, or ova, the female sex cells. The ovaries are located to the right and the left of the uterus, or womb, to which they are connected by the Fallopian tubes.

When a female is born, her ovaries already hold all of the egg cells that will be released during her life. The egg cells do not mature until puberty, when the menstrual cycle begins under the influence of female hormones. In each cycle an egg cell is released. This continues until the menopause, when the menstrual cycle ceases and hormone production is reduced.

The ovaries also produce the female hormones estrogen and progesterone, just as the testes produce testosterone in males. The female hormones circulate throughout the body and keep the sexual system ready for reproduction. The female secretes varying amounts of different hormones in a monthly cycle. During the first half of the cycle, hormones cause a single egg cell to mature and also prepare the lining of the uterus to receive and nourish a fertilized egg; at midcycle, ovulation, or the release of the egg cell from the ovary, takes place. If fertilization and pregnancy do not take place, hormone levels decrease, the lining of the uterus is shed (menstruation, or the monthly period), and the cycle begins again.

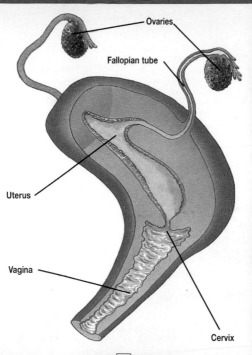

Ovaries

Fallopian tube

Uterus

Vagina

Cervix

REPRODUCTION

The mature egg travels from the ovary to the entrance of the Fallopian tubes, or oviduct and is then transported to the uterus, nourished by sub- stances produced by the Fallopian tubes. This jour- ney takes about three days to complete. Fertilisation – the meeting of egg and sperm – must take place

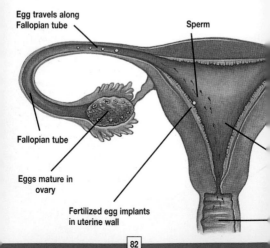

Egg travels along Fallopian tube

Sperm

Fallopian tube

Eggs mature in ovary

Fertilized egg implants in uterine wall

within the Fallopian tube,
It can take place only
within the first 24 hours
of the egg's passage.

The penis contains a large
number of arteries, veins,
small blood vessels and
erectile tissue, which consists of three hollow,
sponge-like cylinders.

When a male has an
erection, these spongy
tissues fill with blood and
become firm, making it
easier to insert the penis
into the vagina. When
ejaculation takes place at
the climax of sexual inter-
course, sperm cells pass
through the urethra and
into the vagina.

Once inside the vagina,
the sperm must make the
journey to the oviduct.
Only a few of the many
millions released will
make it to have a chance
of meeting and fertilising
the egg. If conception
does take place one sperm
will successfully fuse with
the egg to form a zygote.
The zygote contains all
the genetic instructions
needed to form a new
human. As it continues its
journey to the uterus it
begins to divide again and
again and a new life
begins.

Uterus

Vagina

THE FETUS

By the time the zygote reaches the uterus it has become a ball of a hundred or so cells – an embryo. The embryo becomes implanted in the soft lining of the uterus and at this stage it can now be said that the woman is pregnant. For the next 38 weeks or so the embryo will continue to grow, nourished by food received via its mother's blood.

To facilitate the transfer of nutrients from mother to embryo a special organ called the placenta develops from a few of the embryo's cells and becomes fixed to the wall of the uterus. The placenta also allows waste substances to pass from the embryo's blood to the mother's blood.

After four weeks the embryo is 4mm (0.16 inches) long and has already developed a beating heart. By the eighth week the embryo is 46mm (1.8 inches) long and has recognisable arms and legs and a human form. It is now called a fetus. All of the internal organs will have formed by week 12, and by the 16th week the mother may feel the first kicks of the baby.

By week 26 the fetus is around 250mm (10 inches) long and weighs 1.5kg (3lb 5oz), if it is born now it will have a good chance of survival. Over the next weeks the fetus continues to grow. By the time it is born, the baby will be, on average, 360mm (14.5 inches) long and weigh 3.4kg (7lb 8oz).

Fetus

Placenta

Umbilical cord

Although by the time of birth most babies are 'head down' some are in the breech position as here.

BIRTH

The process of giving birth begins with labour, a series of regular contractions of the wall of the uterus brought on by changes in the woman's hormones. Labour is divided into three stages.

The first stage of labour lasts from six to twelve hours and begins with weak regular contractions that gradually get stronger and cause progressive dilatation of the cervix. By the end of this stage the cervix will have opened up to approximately 10cm (4 inches). The head of the baby may break the amnion, the membrane that surrounds the baby in the womb, releasing the protective amniotic fluid, during this stage. This is 'the waters breaking'.

The second stage of labour lasts from one to two hours and begins when the cervix is completely dilated and continues to the birth of the baby. Strong contractions force the baby through the cervix and vagina and out to be born. As soon as the baby starts to breathe the umbilical cord linking it to the placenta will be tied and cut. The baby is now a separate human being in its own right.

The third stage of labour begins with the birth of the baby and continues until the placenta is expelled.

The 'waters breaking', when the baby's head breaks the amnion, is one of the first signs that labour is beginning.

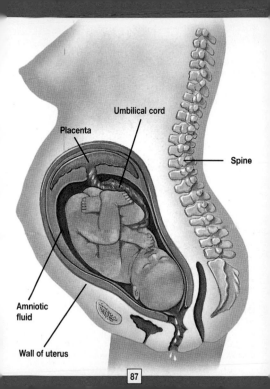

Placenta

Umbilical cord

Spine

Amniotic
fluid

Wall of uterus

GLOSSARY

alveolus: (plural alveoli) one of the many tiny air sacs inside the lungs where carbon dioxide and oxygen are exchanged in breathing.

amnion: The fluid filled sac that surrounds and protects the developing fetus in the womb.

antibodies: Proteins in the blood released by lymphocytes as part of the body's defence mechanisms against bacteria and viruses.

arteries: Blood vessels that carry blood away from the heart to other parts of the body.

atrium: One of the heart's two upper chambers, which receive blood from others parts of the body.

bronchioles: Tiny tubes that carry air to the alveoli.

capillaries: The smallest of the body's blood vessels, carry blood to and from cells and linking arteries to veins to complete the circulatory system.

cell: The basic unit of living organisms. Cells can exist as independent lifeforms, such as bacteria or amoebas, or may form tissues in more complicated organisms, such as humans!

cerebellum: A part of the brain, concerned with equilibrium and movement.

cochlea: The part of the inner ear that contains the sensory organs for hearing.

embryo: The developing baby from the time the fertilized egg is implanted in the lining of the womb until the internal organs begin to form, at which time it is called a fetus.

endocrine glands: Organs of the body that release hormones, the body's chemical messengers, into the bloodstream.

enzyme: Biological catalyst made of protein. Enzymes are classified according to the nature of the substances they act upon and the type of reactions they bring about. Most enzyme names end in -ase, for example lactase breaks down lactose, a form of sugar, proteinases help break down proteins.

fetus: The developing baby from the time the organs form until birth.

gamete: Reproductive cell that joins with another gamete, i.e. an egg and sperm, to develop into an embryo.

glucose: A simple sugar that is the body's principal source of energy.

glycogen: A carbohydrate stored in the liver that can be converted to glucose to meet the body's energy requirements.

haemoglobin: Type of protein found within the red blood cells and giving them their colour. Haemoglobin binds readily with oxygen, allowing more to be transported around the body than would be possible if the gas was simply dissolved in the blood.

hormone: A substance that is manufactured in one part of the body, usually a gland, and released into the bloodstream in very small quantities to be carried to a different part of the body where it will control the activities of the tissues there. Insulin, secreted by the pancreas, is the hormone that controls how glucose is used by the body, for example.

lymphatic system: A system of glands and vessels that drain fluid containing dead cells and bacteria from the tissues of the body, passing it through lymph nodes, which act as cleansing filters.

menstrual cycle: The monthly cycle that takes place in a woman when an egg matures and is released by an ovary and the lining of the womb thickens in preparation to receive it. If the egg is fertilized it will implant in the uterus and the woman is said to be pregnant. If it is not fertilized the lining of the uterus is shed in the monthly 'period'.

metabolism: All the physical and chemical processes that go on within the body. These include building up the constituent parts of the body and breaking down complex molecules to provide energy.

neuron: Another name for a single nerve cell.

organ: A part of the body that performs a particular function. For example, eyes for seeing, lungs for breathing, heart to move blood to the other organs, and so on.

peristalsis: A wave of muscular contractions that move the contents of a tube along, such as the movement of food along the digestive tract.

protein: One of a large group of compounds found in all living things. One particularly important group of proteins, called enzymes, control the rates at which activities take place in cells. The protein keratin gives strength and flexibility to hair, and collagen does the same in skin and tendons. Proteins are an important part of muscles and are involved in the clotting of blood.

reflex: An involuntary response to a stimulus before it has been processed by the brain – as when you jerk your hand away from a hot surface without thinking.

tissue: A group of similar cells organized together to perform a specific function in the body, such as muscle tissue and nerve tissue.

veins: Blood vessels that carry blood to the heart.

ventricles: The two lower chambers of the heart that pump blood back out to the rest of the body.

vitamin: Any of a number of organic compounds required in small amounts by living things to ensure the proper functioning of their cell processes. Vitamins are often necessary to activate certain enzymes.